Bookface

The face of Facebook

Bookface

The face of Facebook

Thought provoking cartoons, insights, and stories about the world's biggest social media site.

Michael Billion

Published by
Billions Worldwide
billionsworldwide@gmail.com
United States of America

Written by Michael Billion

Special thanks to my talented young cartoonist, Shane O' Shaughnessy for the drawings in this book. Your work captured not only the precise images that I outlined for you, but also the spirit and humor of the images. You are awesome.

A special thanks to my developmental editor Michelle Simms-Burton, who shared her exceptional talent with a new author, and who challenged me to be more vulnerable in my writing. This book would not be what it is without you.

Copy editor: Sharon Honeycutt

Cover art: Damir Kundalic

Copy editor: Sharon Honeycutt

Book design & layout: Julie Csizmadia

First Edition

Table of Contents

Preface

In some ways this is actually a book about change, about how the world around us changes and about how we respond to those changes. It attempts to answer the question, "How do we move forward in a changing world and remain true to who we are?" I believe the emergence of Facebook and other social media tools is the most significant cultural shift in our society in decades. In *Bookface,* I explore my own reaction to this new reality and what it means for me.

So in *Bookface* I tell my Facebook story. I realize that hundreds of millions of people also have Facebook stories of their own, and I hope this short book will contribute to that dialogue. I believe we can improve our social media tools and how we use them.

In the book, I also introduce Bookface, the character. He is the personification of the full expression of the new culture being fostered and lead by Facebook. Bookface is a cartoon depiction of a person who lives his or her life as a 100 percent open book. It is a caricature of a person who lives his or her life willing to share everything with everyone, anywhere, and at anytime. That is Bookface.

In *Bookface,* the book, I look at some of the implications of this new culture and how it affects us. I even look at the broader implications of what it means to us when we grant the power of redefining global culture to a for-profit corporation like Facebook, and I invite you to the dialogue. Please enjoy reading *Bookface*. I hope you find it beneficial and entertaining.

Thank you for honoring me with your time and attention.

Acknowledgments

Thank you to my family and all my friends who supported and believed in me as I worked toward the completion of this project. It amazes me how much impact words of encouragement can have upon a person.

I have to especially thank my friends Beatrice, Shafik, Rush, David, Karim, Baye, Jeffrey, Joseph, Terrence, and Marcus for contributing to the publishing of this project. As the saying goes, "Teamwork makes the dream work."

SIR, WOULD YOU LIKE A SIP OF COOL AID?
NO THANKS. I THINK I'LL PASS.

Introduction

What was my problem? Virtually everyone I knew was on Facebook and here I was, the seemingly lone holdout. Everywhere I turned, there it was, Facebook, yet I continued to pass on the opportunity to join. There had to be a real reason. I couldn't accept that I was a tech-adverse old head with irrational apprehensions. Something else was going on. Somewhere there was a story in this that made sense.

I first encountered Facebook in 2006 when a friend of mine, whom I will call "J," had a MySpace page and switched over to using Facebook as a newer alternative. MySpace, he explained, had become too populated by young kids and allowed the users too much creative license to design and manipulate their webpage and their image. He concluded that Facebook was the better alternative because it facilitated communication and connection without all the bells and whistles; therefore it had more integrity and was a more mature group of people. That made sense to me, but I still could hardly see the difference between the two. Aesthetics aside, the only difference I saw was the domain name: J was on Facebook.com instead of MySpace.com.

Within a year or two, Facebook's popularity really took off, and people were signing up by the millions. Occasionally I would run into some of my old friends, and they would often ask me, "Are you on Facebook?" To which I usually replied, "Nah, I really don't have time for that." They would always try to persuade me to join the site by sharing stories about our mutual old friends and how those friends were doing; they were keeping in touch with those folks now. I enjoyed hearing the stories and reconnecting with them, yet somehow the idea of being on the site didn't grab me. Reconnecting with old friends may be a nice thing to do every couple months or maybe even every few years, but every day? So I continued to hold out even though I still didn't understand why. I knew I could connect with friends and family whenever I wanted without Facebook, but if everyone else was joining the site, why shouldn't I? What was the big deal? It seemed I must have some issues. Something must be going on.

Soon Facebook grew to hundreds of millions of users and become the king of social media tools. Businesses everywhere were clamoring to take advantage of the power Facebook offered them—the power to develop a brand and connect with customers, all at little to no cost. People were updating one another, expanding their circle of friends, and reconnecting with others like never before. I wondered just how many ways Facebook could be of use. The possibilities seemed amazing. I began to reconsider whether or not I should join the network. I was beginning to see the light. How might I use Facebook? I asked myself. There was the obvious answer, which was to connect with friends and family, but what else? Well, since I had spent most of my life in service to others and working to make a difference in the world, couldn't I use Facebook to help me make people's lives better? I was sure I could. So why not set up my Facebook page, share my ideas, and utilize Facebook to impact the world? Since Facebook and social media had already changed the world, why not get on board with the social media movement and do the same? Why the hesitation?

I still hadn't really explored why.

Then on May 18, 2012, Facebook announced it would go public. The proposed valuation of the company was $100 billion, and I thought that figure was absurd. How could a company with comparatively little or no real or hard assets be worth so much? At best, I thought the sum was inflated, and at worst, it was a house of cards. I spoke with my oldest son about the Facebook IPO, and I shared with him my belief that it wasn't worth what was projected. During this dialogue about the value of Facebook, I also expressed some of my personal reservations and issues with the social media juggernaut. The more I talked, the more I understood why I had yet to join. Before long I had listed all the reasons why I hadn't joined on a big flip chart. And as I added each reason to the chart, I felt more and more justified in my position. "I knew there was an explanation," I thought to myself. "This thing is not all it's cracked up to be." Then it occurred to me that maybe I should share my thoughts with others. If the ideas were worthwhile, then others could benefit from them.

So I decided to publish my thoughts about Facebook and essentially initiate a written assault against everyone's favorite social media tool. In one little book, I would expose the negative implications of the Facebook culture and bring greater awareness to millions of people. At least, this is what I thought at the time. Maybe it would wind up being social media suicide? But in either case, I got started, and with the use of the dictation capability in my smartphone, I finished dictating and writing the core of all my ideas in about 30 days, which was quite an accomplishment for someone who types very slowly. By early July, I had written my short manuscript and shared it with a few friends. They gave me some useful feedback, but there was a bit of a hush surrounding the direction I was taking the book. "Do you really want to be publicly critical of Facebook?" they asked. Clearly it was a socially risky endeavor, yet in spite of my apprehensions, I made some modifications and pressed on.

It wasn't until I shared the manuscript with my editor that my real issues came to light. After reading my manuscript, she told me she was ready to give me the feedback I needed. I expected to see red ink everywhere: misspelled words, grammatical errors, corrections on sentence structure, and more. Surprisingly none of this was really the case. Instead, in this first session, she took an entirely different direction. She asked me, "Where are you in this book?"

"What?" I thought to myself. "The book is not about me. It's about Facebook," I answered.

She responded, "Yeah, well, your readers need to hear a story, and they need to feel connected to your story. You are critiquing Facebook, but the question is who is going to care about what you think if there is no story to it?"

"Ouch," I thought, but I saw her point. I began to reflect about why I was hesitant to put myself in the book when it would make for a better read. The question reminded me of another contradiction: I had not yet joined Facebook in spite of its obvious use in facilitating my goals. Now I was forced to look at myself in the mirror, and I felt a little insecure. Reluctantly, I had to admit to myself that the thought of opening up and sharing my life with people online made me uncomfortable, and the same was apparently true of sharing my story in the book.

Over the years I had grown to accept that I am a fairly private person who lives a fantastic life, and I saw no reason to mess with what worked. Why open myself up online to the world when it seems to only distract, add little value, and could possibly cause some problems? Because everyone else was doing it? I couldn't see the point. But here I was facing very good reasons to open up online and in the book, and yet I was still hesitant. So my editor asked me to explore my feelings and challenged me to allow myself to be more vulnerable by expressing my apprehensions in the book as part of my story and by possibly creating a Facebook page. Wow. Her response really set me back. The process which began as a social critique of Facebook and—to an extent—of social media, ended up being a very personal and introspective process. I thought the book was essentially finished, and instead she had turned the tables on me. I was now exploring my own inner hang-ups. What the heck?

What is really going on here? I thought. Do I actually have a hang-up? The more I thought about it, I realized I could no longer avoid the obvious. I had to conclude that, yes, I had a hang-up. But what precisely was it? After taking some time away from the book to reflect on my new insights and on my life, and after talking it through with friends, it finally hit me. My issue was a fear of receiving public attention. I did not like the public spotlight. Whether it was due to a view that calling attention to me was ignoble and self-centered or whether it was just plain old insecurity, receiving public attention had always made me uncomfortable. In high school, I was a pretty good basketball player in parks, yet I didn't shine as I should have in my high school games. As an adult, in my professional life and service work, I always found ways to make the maximum impact while bringing a minimal amount of attention to myself. I handled the attention when I played the role of a subordinate member of a team because it was a supporting role. I even took the lead when the activity I was engaged in was a social cause because the cause was the focus, not me and my achievements. The more I thought about it, the more I could see it. My aversion to the spotlight had always been there. I had made a life out of ducking the spotlight. And because Facebook was essentially one's own personal spotlight shining so that the entire world could see you, I understood now why it would strike a nerve in me. My issue with Facebook was an aversion to the spotlight and not simply some grand social critique as I would have liked to believe.

This presented an enormous problem for me because I realized that as the use of online tools like Facebook became the new culture of the world, I would have to make a choice as to whether or not to participate. And my choice hinged on one question,

"Can you influence and significantly impact the lives of others with your ideas without calling attention to yourself and without the use social media tools like Facebook?" The obvious answer was "Not really," and even if it were possible, what a challenge that would be. Facebook and other social media tools are here to stay and to further evolve our society. If I am to fulfill what I believe to be my purpose in life, I would have to open up and embrace these new tools and the change they bring.

It is far better that I face and overcome my hang-ups than expend energy going against the tide. Rather than swim upstream, why not join the fray, share my ideas, and influence people using the new social media tools? It was time I man up and take the necessary steps. I would publish *Bookface,* and in it, I would tell my story and still offer my critique. *Bookface* is both of those things. At its core, *Bookface* is my analysis of how our lives are transformed by Facebook in ways we may not see, yet it is also quite personal. In the end, it offers ways to engage Facebook in a responsible way.

Upon the suggestion of my friend Jeff, I added questions at the end of each chapter to make it a tool for self-reflection. In response to my friend Beatrice's suggestion that I include images, I created original cartoon artwork to illustrate my ideas. Being a bit of a comedian, I had to inject humor to help make my points, so I hope you find the book humorous at times. Maybe reading it will even stimulate dialogue and self-reflection, as it did for me.

In the end, I'm sure there are many people who will think my analysis of Facebook is an example of overthinking something that is really quite simple. To them I say that I completely understand. But as someone who appreciates the depth and complexity of each and every human being, I wrote this piece as my way of going on record to say that we are more than a Bookface.

I hope you enjoy reading the book.

I HAVE NEVER BEEN ONE TO WASTE TIME.
FEB 2112
FACEBOOK

CHAPTER ONE

Time Waster

"The average Facebook user spends 636 minutes per month on Facebook."
- FACEBOOK OCT. 2013 (THIS IS EQUIVALENT TO THREE FULL TIME WORK WEEKS PER YEAR.)

"The average Facebook user spends 20 minutes on the site per visit."
- INFOGRAPHICS LAB 2012

I saw this very funny video clip on YouTube of a woman named Sweet Brown who was being interviewed by a reporter, and who said at the end of her interview, "Ain't nobody got time for that!" That statement summed up how I first felt about Facebook. I recall being with a friend who showed me his Facebook page, and it was full of postings from "friends" about the most trivial and simple topics you could imagine. I thought, "Are you kidding me? Do I really want to hear what you ate last night? Or how you felt about some TV show?" It was surprising to me how much time people were spending writing and reading such material.

When I mentioned my thoughts to my buddy, he said, "Yeah I know. There is a lot of junk, but you don't have to read it all. Just scroll down and read the ones that are important to you." So I watched him do it, and I concluded it was still silly and a waste of time. Looking at his Facebook wall felt like I was reading the side wall in a bathroom stall, scrolling through a bunch of random remarks looking for the something of redeeming value. Well okay, maybe it wasn't quite that bad, but you get the point. I couldn't imagine myself spending time every day sifting through all that rubbish for a few remotely relevant comments, trying to convince myself it was worthwhile when it was really a colossal waste of my time. In my mind, Sweet Brown was right. "Ain't nobody got time for that!" I don't even watch commercials I don't like, so how could I read through all those random remarks? There has to be a better way. If I am to use Facebook, I have to find a way to extract the value without subjecting myself to endless chatter.

Questions:

1. Do you ever feel like you don't have enough time in the day to do what you need to do?

2. Do you feel you spend too much time on Facebook?

3. Do you see any consequences for all the time people spend on Facebook?

FACEBOOK

CHAPTER TWO

Distraction

Right now I'm walking in a local park in my neighborhood. It is Mother's Day, Sunday morning, families are out, children are playing, birds are chirping, and it is absolutely a gorgeous day. I can't help but be overcome by the beauty of this moment.

Here is my point. I cannot replicate this online. But I can miss it if I spend all my free time on Facebook—or simply online for that matter. Regardless of one's circumstances, there is always something to experience. There is something to enjoy, something to laugh about, or something to see, and most importantly there is always so much to do. As a result, there is a need to be present in one's life, if not for enjoyment, then for survival and success.

We live in challenging times. People are facing challenges in their finances, health, relationships, and more. The world is transforming so rapidly that many are struggling just to keep up. We are faced with so many personal and collective problems that need solutions that it begs these questions, "Where should you put your attention—on making the most of your real life or on a virtual one? Do you actually think they are the same?"

To me, getting caught up on Facebook seems like a distraction from the real world and the things I want to do in life (as if I don't already have enough distractions). I already feel as if I don't have enough time to accomplish the things I would like to do. Truth be told, I watch too much television as it is. Setting up digital relationships with everyone I know would siphon quality time and attention from my actual life and my real world-real time relationships. I fear it is a slippery slope upon which the first encounter is harmless, but over time those little digitized sessions would gradually increase, ultimately distracting me from my responsibilities, consuming my mind with the insignificant, and leveraging everyone I know to pull me into an online world and away from the physical one in which I live. It's difficult enough to stay mentally sharp in this world of media snippets and excessive entertainment and gossip; why adopt a new virtual world of lightweight relationships and trivial activity?

I wonder if Facebook is a big escape from real-life situations and problems. One friend confided in me that his girlfriend, who is an exceptionally smart director of a high-profile organization, uses Facebook and other media sites as a way of detaching from her real-life responsibilities. And although I can see the benefit in doing that, the truth is I already have distractions built into my life to help me detach, zone out, and clear my head. I don't need new methods. Besides, joining everyone I know in that kind of activity just might end up consuming me. My viewpoint regarding Facebook has been like rap star/music mogul Jay-Z's, who said in a rhyme once regarding social media, "No I never been on MySpace too busy let my voice vibrate." With all of my responsibilities and goals, if I allow Facebook to distract me, I am done! So "I'm focused man."

Questions:

1. Do you think Facebook is a distraction?

2. Do you enjoy Facebook as a welcomed distraction?

3. Is there a consequence for being distracted? If so, what is it?

FACEBOOK
FACEBOOK
FACEBOOK
FACEBOOK
FACEBOOK
MIGHT WE BE
ADDICTED?

CHAPTER THREE

Habit Forming

It never occurred to me that someone could become a Facebook addict until my friend, who is a very successful professional, admitted to me that he had become one. He confided that he was spending hours a day on Facebook—reading comments, responding to posts, checking his Facebook page all day—even while at work. He was addicted, and I'm sure his wife and kid weren't too fond of it, nor was his employer. But fortunately for him, somehow over time he decided to kick the habit. He "de-friended" a few hundred people and cut back on his usage. He Facebook detoxed, and luckily Facebook doesn't leave tracks on its users' arms or he would have been in trouble. This friend of mine was strong enough to pull back and see the impact of his addiction, yet I had to ask myself, "Do I really need another bad habit?"

The thought of becoming a Facebook addict was a bit unnerving to me, especially because I have so many people that I know I can connect with through Facebook. My apprehensions intensified when I learned that another one of my very good friends, whom I respect as being uber smart, proudly told me he was addicted to Facebook and that he spends 12 or more hours a day checking in on the site. He, in contrast to my other friend, continues to use the site excessively. I found his usage rate to be unbelievable and a bit scary. I thought to myself, "Could I get caught up like that? And my answer was, "Maybe." So what should I do? Say no to digital drugs? Yes. For me to be on Facebook, it would have to serve my purpose, and my purpose doesn't involve me becoming a Facebook junkie.

Questions:

1. Do you think Facebook can be addictive?
2. What behaviors would someone have to have for you to consider him or her a Facebook addict?
3. Do you or does anyone you know have a Facebook addiction?
4. Does being a Facebook addict have any consequences?
5. What are the consequences of being a Facebook addict?

COME ON!
OPEN UP AND SHARE!
WE DID!
BUT IT FEELS A LITTLE WEIRD.

CHAPTER FOUR

Peer Pressure

I really thought adults outgrew peer pressure after high school, yet here it was rearing its ugly head again, beginning with the peer pressure I felt to join Facebook. As I watched my friends use Facebook, the peer pressure dynamic was everywhere, and it was laughable. My friends and I would be sitting somewhere and people would post questions on their page for others to respond to—questions that in truth my friends felt were ridiculous. But because their "friends" were involved, they felt compelled to respond.

And not only did they respond, they didn't even give their honest answers. In most cases they gave answers they felt would be acceptable to the group, not what they actually thought. When I saw this, I thought to myself, "Are they being phony?" No, I didn't think they were being phony; instead, I viewed it as being considerate of others. I soon realized they were editing their responses because so many other people were reading their responses. They couldn't answer the questions as they would have if they had been talking to an individual because their entire peer network was witnessing the conversation. As a result, an unnecessary and weird form of peer pressure emerged that shaped all their responses. This peer pressure compels people to self-edit their responses so that they are consistent with their perception of the groups' perception. It doesn't get much stranger than that.

This peer pressure also compels people to post pictures and make remarks based on what they feel their network would like. Meanwhile, they don't post many of the things that are actually occurring in their lives or thoughts they actually share with folks in the "real world" because (it seems to me) it doesn't fit the online, big-group culture. Are all of these folks psychologically weak for being influenced by peer pressure? No, they are not. It is natural for people who are being monitored by a large group that they hold in high regard to acquiesce to the group's point of view. It is the impact of Facebook's design that creates the peer pressure. The site promotes responding, sharing, and connecting; however, with its voyeuristic design, it also creates an environment where people are self-conscious and feel compelled to heavily self-edit their content. This leads to the emergence of peer pressure and the urge to always be acceptable and agreeable to your "all-seeing" group.

It also appears that Facebook leverages this peer pressure by encouraging people to share more, which in turn increases the value of the site. More sharing means more data and more time spent on the site, and more data and time on the site ultimately results in more revenue for Facebook. Although I find none of this peer-pressure manipulation appealing, I will find a way to use the site without being manipulated in ways I don't want to be.

Question:

1. Do you see peer pressure influencing people in group settings or on online social networks like Facebook? If so,explain.

2. Do you see peer pressure affecting people on Facebook? If so, how are they being affected?

3. Do you ever feel peer pressure on Facebook or other social networks? If so, explain.

PROFESSOR, WHAT ARE YOU DOING?
I'M RESPONDING TO A FACEBOOK POSTING OF A FARTING DOG!
LOL

CHAPTER FIVE

Dumbing Down

Without mentioning it to my friends, I actually thought they were dumbing down while on Facebook. I didn't think they or their "friends" were actually dumb, but that in order to say something everyone would generally like, they had to say something simple. They had to share something that would appeal to the least common denominator of the group to find widespread acceptance, something like "Man, it's hot outside. LOL." They needed to make simple comments that were generally acceptable and agreeable so that everyone could respond. I even felt a little silly when just reading over their page.

Ironically, I knew that the people posting were rather intelligent, but here was this website making everyone speak and act in ways they ordinarily would not. The need to find acceptance and agreement was actually dumbing them down online. Watching these intelligent people adjust themselves and their communication in order to fit in with their Facebook group was a turn off. Could I become a part of the Facebook community without feeling like I was dumbing down? Certainly I would find a way. I'm sure I'm not the only one who had these concerns.

Questions:

1. Do you see people dumbing down on Facebook? If so, explain.

2. Can you think of times when you have dumbed down on Facebook, either through what you have shared or how you responded to something?

3. If so, can you answer why you did it?

4. Do you think while on Facebook or other social media sites, people tend to respond more to comments or postings that are trivial, negative, or sensational?

FACEBOOK DOESN'T CHANGE US.

CHAPTER SIX
Homogenization

After looking at one friend's site, I asked myself, who was the person she represented online? It certainly was not the individual I knew. The person I knew rarely engaged in idle chatter and even disliked it. But on Facebook, she was different. She joined the chatter. That is obviously no big deal, but I was curious about the difference. When I asked, she said that it was just the group's culture on Facebook. My conclusion was that Facebook was homogenizing people. Though relatively innocent, it was making everyone the same. The true individual others experience in the real world is often not represented online. Instead, when on Facebook, people seem to become an oversimplified and more agreeable version of themselves—a fact that I concluded was a result of the site's functional design.

Here is how I think it works: It begins with the so-called "privacy settings." How can something be private when your entire network reads it? The reality is on Facebook, "private" generally means "public," more specifically a limited public (your network). A person's newsfeed and wall are in actuality public and not private, and they influence people to be self-conscious when they post because they know their entire network is watching. In essence, they know "private" still means "public." This self-consciousness leads to self-editing as people try to post and respond in ways they feel the group would like. As a result, a neutral Facebook persona emerges among the group because everyone is trying to please the group. Consequently, the complexity and reality of each wonderfully dynamic individual is completely lost. Like reducing fractions in grade school math, people end up being reduced to the least common denominator of the group, a sort of basic, acceptable Facebook persona.

My thought regarding this was, "Why should I reduce myself? Why reduce a Billion? (Pun intended!) And what am I reducing myself to?" Do I want to become a person who communicates online with his "Facebook friends" in a way that is inauthentic yet agreeable to them all? For many people, they could care less, but for me, being true to myself is important. If I am to join Facebook, I will have to find a way to be true to myself without distancing myself from others. That could prove challenging.

Question:

1. If you knowingly have a group of people watching you and your behavior, do you think that would affect you at all?

2. If so, how would it affect you?

3. Have you observed that when on Facebook people tend to sound the same or very similar?

Time + Sharing = Friends = Popular

CHAPTER SEVEN

Artificial Social Hierarchy

My observations of Facebook users led me to conclude that sharing puts you in the in- crowd. It is as if, the more you post, the higher up the social hierarchy you go. And the more time you spend on the site, the more likely you are to share and accumulate more "friends." Before you know it, you are cool and popular; you're a star. You are the focal point of everyone that you know, while in reality you might be able to count the number of friends you actually have on one hand, which leads me to wonder: Is a tool like Facebook a magnet for cornballs who want to achieve social popularity without actually being socially competent? Isn't it true that if people really like you, you will naturally accumulate friends? You don't have to share every thought, every action, every picture, and every detail about your life in order to become popular and liked. It is unnecessary. Just be yourself and live life; the friends come with it. It seems these days the need people feel for validation and acceptance has led to a stampede of people sharing too much information.

Questions:

1. Have you ever observed people on Facebook whom you felt were sharing or adding friends to try to appear popular or cool?

2. Have you ever seen someone who was really popular on Facebook but not so popular in the "real" world?

3. Do you think Facebook facilitates an exaggerated or false sense of popularity?

CHAPTER EIGHT

Daily Nostalgia?

Did I have a blast in high school? Yes. But like many others, I also hated it at times. Do I want to relive it? No, I was happy when I left. And ultimately that's how I view my past. The past is called "the past" for a reason. It's over. The past exists in memories and photos. So to me, the only folks who are trying to relive the past are people who think their best days are behind them; therefore, they are not excited about their future. My past was awesome, but so is my present. I'm having a ball now, so why would I get caught up in old stuff?

Many of the folks using Facebook are excited about reconnecting with old friends, which often means school-age friends, and thus their Facebook conversation is often nostalgic. I too enjoy reconnecting with old friends; it is amazing to see how things change over time, but I am careful not to confuse my past with my present. My past was more or less the result of my upbringing and my circumstances, but my current life is more the result of my choices. If I spend too much time looking backward, it gives my past too much control over my present and limits my future. Change happens for a reason. The past is in the past because people and circumstances have changed. Everything has evolved. I can't allow my future to be unduly influenced by over-reminiscing about the past. I firmly believe that (daily) overexposure to your past influences you such that you end up making your future more like your past, and I refuse to let that happen. As much as I love old friends, old memories, and my past, I can't go backwards; I have to keep it moving. Facebook's design keeps everyone from your past directly in front of you and in direct communication with you and with your entire network. This is a blending of past and present that gives the past even more power over your present and your future than it naturally has.

Besides, having every friend and acquaintance I have ever met in my life staring at me online every day seems a bit creepy. It's nice to connect every now and then, but I don't live in the past. Nor do I want to hear what everyone I have ever met has to say on a daily basis. Life is in the present. I will keep it that way.

On another note, I take issue with melding all my relationships and collapsing my life's timeline in way that everyone I know—past and present—is all in the same place, communicating with me and with each other. I think it is a form of social network deconstruction. Life doesn't actually work that way, so why should I? All my relationships exist in a certain time and space, and generally I like to keep it that way.

Questions:

1. Do you find yourself being more nostalgic when on Facebook?

2. Do you think your best days are behind you?

3. Do you think focusing on the past can influence your present and ultimately your future?

I'M TRYING TO ADD FRIENDS. YOU GUYS SHOULD JUST WAIT!
FACEBOOK
FRIENDS

CHAPTER NINE

"Friends"

In the mid-1980s, a rap group named Whodini had a smash hit called "Friends." The chorus of the song went like this:

Friends,
How many of us have them?
Friends,
Ones you can depend on.
Friends

That's similar to how I view friends, dependable. Call me old-fashioned, but a mouse click is not really a relationship and certainly not a friendship. Each of my relationships is distinct and has meaning. And what the relationship means to me is not necessarily what it means to the other person. So how could Facebook facilitate all that meaning, diversity, and distinction when it reduces relationships to public postings and to very limited digital expressions? It seems it might devalue or redefine even my most basic relationships.

Also, my friends are very diverse. Some of my friends would not really "click" with others who are my friends. That's just how real life works. Each relationship is personalized, dynamic, and distinct. No two relationships are the same. So if I have all of these distinct and complex relationships, how can I just meld them all into the same place, at the same time, and communicate with all of them in the same way? Would I even want them hearing what each of the others had to say? Not really.

Relationships are accumulated over time, and each is very unique. I wonder if using Facebook will collapse my relationships' web into a blob, where everyone I know is in the same place, in real time, communicating in ways that are a bit untrue to who they actually are. If so, that would be a form of network deconstruction. Relationships help to define a certain period in a person's history, so to collapse the relationships' web is to collapse a person's story. And even if a person's story and history exist only in their mind, they still define who that person is and how they view themselves. Again, collapsing the relationships' web collapses the complexity of the individual.

Consider too being faced with the option of rejecting "friends," or even worse, "de-friending" a friend. In the real world you don't "de-friend" a friend; you just move on. The relationship is no longer active, but the friend isn't rejected. If I am to be a part of Facebook, I have to do so without adversely affecting my relationships. Is that even possible?

Questions:

1. How many actual friends do you think you have?

2. How many Facebook "friends" do you have?

3. Does your number of real-life friends match your number of Facebook "friends"?

4. Do you spend enough time with your actual friends in person?

5. Do you spend more time with your friends on Facebook or in person?

nah.
WILL YOU BE MY FRIEND?

CHAPTER TEN

I'm Too Cool

Okay, on a more lighthearted note, I have to ask myself, "Is Facebook kind of corny?" And although I won't go so far as to call Facebook corny, I do think it gets close at times. I had many friends while in grade school. I was rather popular as a teenager too. In college, I was also well known. But the thing is, with all of that popularity, I don't ever remember actually asking anyone to be my friend. There's just something juvenile about that. Friendship was something that happened because it was mutually earned. It seems corny and awkward to ask for and accumulate "friends" through mouse clicks, even if you already know the person.

Also, getting my friendship offer denied or avoided is definitely not cool. I'm not overly sensitive about this because my self-concept doesn't depend on it, but I don't enjoy being snubbed, even if it's digital. A digital diss is still a diss. If I were on Facebook, I would expect acceptance of my digital hand in friendship, even if I reject or ignore someone else's.

Another thing that infringes upon my cool is participating in circuses with people who share information that folks aren't interested in receiving, which appears to be the norm for many on Facebook. "Can we have select sharing, people? No ***oversharing,*** please!" Everyone doesn't want to know everything you are thinking and doing. I hold that if a person would not share something with me face-to-face, they should not share it with me in our digitized relationship on Facebook. Furthermore, if something is shared online, maybe it is best to share it with me in private, or in a private group like communication occurs in the real world. That seems much more practical than on a public wall where everyone I have ever known is watching. Sharing things with the wrong people or with a group that is too broad is actually ***mis-sharing*** and it is not a good thing. Everyone knows that a group of guys may say something to each other in private that would not always be suitable for a broader group. Because people communicate on a public wall and through public newsfeeds, Facebook's design encourages people to communicate in ways that are not only strange but prone to cause conflict and misunderstandings. I think the site's design may promote mis-sharing and oversharing, both of which are definitely problematic.

As a result, I have to ask myself, "Can Facebook be customized to suit me and my concerns, or will I transform myself and my communication to fit in with the general Facebook culture?" I could probably extend that question to other social media tools as well. Of course, many people will be quick to point out that the Facebook privacy settings give you control over what is shared and accessed, but they miss the point about culture and design, both of which influence behavior. I guess if I am to join Facebook, I will have to work that one out, but in the meantime I know that oversharing and mis-sharing are no-no's.

Questions:

1. Have you ever had any awkward moments on Facebook?

2. Have you ever witnessed people oversharing or mis-sharing on Facebook?

3. Have you ever overshared or mis-shared on Facebook?

4. What was the consequence of oversharing or mis-sharing?

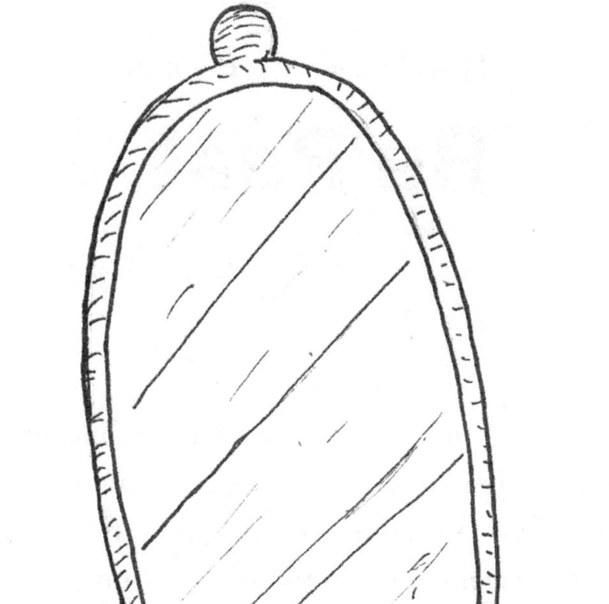

IS THAT REALLY YOU?

CHAPTER ELEVEN

Be Real

I recall hearing a story of a woman who, while on vacation with a friend, staged pictures to upload on her Facebook page to make their trip appear more fun than it actually was. Everywhere they went she was pulling random men into their pictures—along with bottles of liquor they hadn't drunk—to create a false impression. I guess creating an online persona of yourself that is not real is a tempting impulse when you have a Facebook page, and many people can't resist. It prompted me to ask myself, "What do I think about those who deliberately post inauthentic information?" The guy who posts a picture of himself in front of a Ferrari he doesn't own and tries to pass it off as though it is his. The girl who posts a 10-year-old picture of herself as though it is current because the picture conveniently hides the forty pounds she has gained. Unfortunately, I have seen many a fakery online, a caricature of the real person. Online, the most socially lame among us can become the smartest and coolest. As such it is not uncommon to see people stage photos for the sole purpose of creating an image on Facebook. It is a false persona. The strange thing is though, when everyone is sharing to create an impression rather than sharing what actually is, it creates a mass illusion. This may explain why it appears on Facebook that everyone's life is so full of highlights and insights that it makes you wonder if real-world challenges even exist. When reading over people's Facebook pages, it appears that nearly everyone is a virtual Beyonce, Jay Z, Oprah, Tony Robbins, or Joel Osteen. Everyone is a beacon of knowledge and wisdom and an example of personal triumph. My perception is that the online environment allows people to be their idealized self rather than their actual self.

This means that often when you communicate with someone in an online environment like Facebook, you are not actually communicating directly with people; you are more or less communicating with their created persona. This phenomenon of an idealized persona leads me to the next thought ... surrogates.

Questions:

1. How close to the "real you" is your online or Facebook persona?

2. How close to their actual personas are the online personas of your "friends"?

HI! I WOULD LIKE TO GET TO KNOW YOU!
SEE ME ON FACEBOOK. I'M MUCH BETTER ONLINE.
BUS STOP

CHAPTER TWELVE

Surrogates

I recall watching this movie called *Surrogates* starring Bruce Willis a few years back. At the time it seemed like some sort of far-out sci-fi film with no connection to our current society. The movie was about people who sat in their homes and lived their lives through these almost human cyber robots. The people never left the comfort of their home, but rather they experienced every aspect of life, (emotions, touch, etc.) and lived in the real world through their cyber robot. They lived like this to wall themselves off from pain and difficulty, while also maintaining the appearance of youth, beauty, and personal perfection through their surrogate (cyber robot). Everyone's cyber robot looked amazing; however, in the reality of the movie, the people were merely sitting at home in chairs, hooked up electronically through their brains to a digital network that allowed them to control and experience life through their human-like cyber robot's body. Everything that people did in real life, these cyber robot users did using their surrogates. The film was similar to *The Matrix* in that everyone was wired in, and everyone was online in a complex web of relationships and experiences that were experienced only in their minds.

As farfetched and absurd as it might appear, I see Facebook as a very tiny step in that direction. It is possible that, much like Alexander Graham Bell is credited with creating the first telephone over a hundred years ago, in the future Mark Zuckerberg and his Facebook team could be credited with creating the first significant virtual world where people could actually live. Maybe we are slowly approaching *The Matrix* or the use of surrogates. Maybe one's profile and Facebook page are merely the earliest precursors of one's surrogate self. I know it's a crazy thought, but virtual reality is an evolving technology. Yet even if the idea of someday having virtual surrogates is dismissed as a wacky sci-fi dream, then consider this: "Is a real relationship equivalent to observing a two-dimensional blinking image of someone?" Can I "feel" someone on Facebook and not in the physical sense? Isn't there a huge difference between being physically in someone's presence and communicating with them, and communicating with a two-dimensional digital representation of them?

I have a friend who was dating a guy long-distance that she knew from high school. They recently reconnected and were communicating regularly on Facebook. Interestingly, on Facebook this guy was the life of the party. He was funny, smart, witty, interesting, insightful, sexy, and conversational—the total package. Yet the more they connected in the real world, the more she began to know him and not his "online surrogate." When she was in his actual presence, she felt he was a lot less appealing.

All the slick words he could muster while typing on a screen (or even texting) he couldn't quite deliver on the spot in the real world. Although they had fun doing different activities, the truth is, in person he could not measure up to his Facebook persona. He was more appealing online than in real life, and I wouldn't be surprised if he felt the same about her.

Sadly, it is possible that the more people practice creating an awesome persona online, the more likely they are to disappoint others in the real world. This may be true because staring at a screen is not real life; it merely reinforces the habit of isolation while giving the illusion of real connections and authentic experiences. As a result of living through the surrogates in the film *Surrogates,* the actual people using the surrogates began to atrophy, gain weight, age ungracefully, and lose their ability to socially navigate and experience the real world. I hope we are not heading in the same direction as a consequence of having chosen to settle for a limited digital playhouse as our means of relating to the world. "Digital Barbie, meet digital Ken."

Questions:

1. Have you ever witnessed or experienced people using exaggerated or idealized online personas or "surrogates" on Facebook?

2. How do you feel about people representing themselves on Facebook as a grander version of themselves?

3. Is your online persona a better or enhanced version of who you are?

4. Does it even matter if someone's online persona is an enhanced version of themselves?

5. If so, why does it matter?

CHAPTER THIRTEEN

The Real Me

How could I actually represent myself online? I, like many people, am actually way too dynamic for that. I'm not bragging—it is just true. I have met so many people. I have had so many experiences, and I have accumulated just too much information over the years to actually represent it all online. Each of my relationships is uniquely nuanced and has different conversations and experiences associated with it. The complexity of these relationships and experiences is the reality of who I am and of my life. This is not just true for me; it is true for everyone. All of us can only post very small pieces of who we are, glimpses of whatever piece we choose to share. In reality, our posts are only a very tiny fraction of who we actually are.

Also, we relate to others differently to some extent, depending upon our relationship to them. This complexity gets confused when everyone is communicating in a group context because we end up communicating with everyone in the same way. Do we communicate with our closest friends the way we communicate with our colleagues at work? Because there is a difference in how and what we communicate with different people, why should our Facebook interactions be any different? I have to ask myself this question: "If my communication with someone is specific and customized, how can I share things that are both what I want to say and authentic, yet remain true to how I actually communicate with each person, while others are observing? It can be quite awkward. It seems Facebook's design leads users to communicate on a wall or through a newsfeed as if all communication is the same, and I find that a bit strange. Are we all bathroom poets, writing general messages on walls for people to read?

To me the site's design looks like a recipe for relationship confusion. So how should I handle it? Maybe Facebook works best as a personal broadcast station? Since I could use one, I will have to take that under serious consideration.

Questions:

1. How much of who you actually are should be represented online or on Facebook?

2. Do you think it is possible to share or represent all of who you are online or on Facebook?

3. Do you try to represent all of who you are on online or on Facebook?

SHOWTIME

CHAPTER FOURTEEN

The Truman Show

"We are building a web where the default setting is social," Mark Zuckerberg, Facebook founder and CEO, declared in 2010. It means that in the culture of Facebook, virtually everything in your life is meant to be shared. You are encouraged to become a completely open book, a Bookface. It reminds me of another movie I saw called *The Truman Show* starring Jim Carrey. Truman was this guy whose life from inception to adulthood was entirely conceived of and filmed as a reality television show. Everyone in his life was actually an actor, and everything in his life was just a prop on a movie set. The humor of the show is that Truman, whose life was the hottest show on television, did not know his life was a television show. He thought he was simply living and that his relationships and experiences were real, while in reality they were a script that was being followed by paid actors and he was being recorded and filmed unknowingly. Only his show was real, and it was being viewed by millions of people. *The Truman Show* reminds me of Facebook.

Like in *The Truman Show,* the Facebook directive goes like this: Put your entire life on your Facebook page, and because the default setting is social, remember to share everything. Put it on a timeline and involve everyone you have ever known. Lay it out in vivid detail; use photos, use videos, use music, tell the story, and leave nothing out. You too can have a reality TV show; like Truman, you too can be a star! Well, personally speaking, I don't like the idea of sharing everything. In fact, I fundamentally disagree with the idea. My life is meant to be experienced, not watched online—especially if I am not being paid for it. Does that mean I don't want to share my life experiences with others? Absolutely not. It means that I share them with select people and in person whenever I am able because, for me, sharing in person is a fun experience.

When I have an experience I want to share, I enjoy telling the story in person. In fact, telling the story in person is often better than the experience itself. My friends and family love sharing stories, pictures, and experiences in person. Our moments of sharing in person are so rewarding they are experiences in and of themselves. Should I take a picture of myself telling stories of an experience to friends so that I can put the picture of the storytelling experience online? Gets a little twisted, I believe. I prefer to tell the story in person where we can feel and embrace the moment, the interactions, and the emotions. Only in person can I feel the full enjoyment of sharing with friends and family. The experience of typing "lmao" is not even remotely close to actually laughing my ass off in person with my friends. Online sharing is very useful, but I think it only complements real-life sharing. Nothing beats the real world and nothing is better than the real you.

Besides, my life is mine. I share what I want, only with whom I want, when I want, and how I want to share it. And a culture where everything is social is contrary to that. Now, does my refusal to be an open book online mean that something is up or that something is wrong with me? Absolutely not. I have never been one to be a blabbermouth about all my personal details. In fact, I can recall feeling a little uncomfortable as a kid when my mom (bless her heart) would occasionally make small talk with strangers by sharing some details of my life and what I was doing. Though I now know she was merely making small talk, at the time I would think to myself, "Who are they that she needs to tell them what I'm doing?"

The reality is, I generally only share what I want to, based on what I feel is right for that particular relationship, at that moment in time. For me, the default setting is not social; the default setting is "appropriate." Strictly speaking, the directive should actually be: "Share what is appropriate or best at that time, for that particular person." I'm not going to express my basketball opinions for my mom to read because Mark Zuckerberg says the default setting is social.

Nor will I allow myself to be subtly manipulated by peer pressure and Facebook's default settings to compromise my values and become someone I am not. This again is a reality many Facebook users fail to see, the influence of design on behavior and culture. If a group of people walk into a large room that has two sofas facing each other and a chair off in the corner, they will likely congregate around the sofas and move the chair to the sofas. Very few individuals will go sit in the chair alone while the group sits on the sofas. It is basic group behavior, and the functional design of the site and its default settings will determine the culture, not an individual's choice. The individual will decide only whether they are in the main crowd or not.

So how can I continue to be true to my values and still utilize Facebook? For starters, I will do my best to share what is appropriate and authentic. And I hope my life's story doesn't devolve into *The Truman Show*, especially if someone else is profiting from my life's content.

Questions:

1. How do you feel about people having their private lives on display?

2. Do you like having your life online for public or semi-public view?

3. Have you developed an appetite for watching the private lives of others?

LOOK AT THIS PICTURE I POSTED!
THIS GUY IS CRAZY!
HE'S A WEIRDO!
JUDGING MADE EASY

CHAPTER FIFTEEN

Judgment

There is a popular expression that goes, "Only God can judge a person"; if only that were true. In reality, everyone can and does judge people. I guess the actual point of that expression is that only God is qualified to judge a person.

As an observer of different personal Facebook pages, I couldn't help but see how easy it was to pass judgment on someone. It seemed that by observing snippets of information and personal pictures and thoughts—all posted without much context or explanation—I, like many others, was prone to judge. Receiving bits of information about people and their lives out of context produces judgment. I recall the collective reaction of some friends when they saw racy pictures posted by their Facebook girlfriend who was apparently having a "moment." It changed their view of her and their view of the folks who responded favorably to her posting. Funny thing is, I'm sure the woman wouldn't just walk up to all those folks and whip those pictures out, but Facebook made sharing so easy and so broad that it lent itself to oversharing and mis-sharing and thus created judgment.

Another observable fact is that when someone is looking in on the details of another person's life as though they are watching a reality show, it actually stimulates the urge to comment and gossip about them. It urges the person to pass judgment. That's ultimately what the comment section on Facebook is for. Just pay attention to people's reactions when they observe or hear the details of what is going on in someone's life. They pass judgment and make comments. But doesn't commenting and gossiping about other people's lives seem immature? Facebook's culture seems so much like high school behavior. Just like in high school, you have people who are doing and saying things to impress the crowd, all while gossiping about the crowd at the same time.

The petty tendency to judge and gossip about the lives of others is not a personal characteristic I want to develop in myself, nor do I want my life to be someone else's gossip material. It is unfortunate, though, that gossiping and passing judgment on others has become an American pastime.

Question:

1. Have you ever judged someone negatively or misperceived them based on their online communication or persona?

2. Have you ever felt misperceived or judged negatively based on something you shared online?

3. What can be done to limit misperception, misunderstanding, and judgment online?

DIVORCE COURT
LET ME GUESS... YOU SAW EACH OTHER'S FACEBOOK PAGE?

CHAPTER SIXTEEN

Conflict

One of the inevitable consequences of Facebook's culture is conflict. Oversharing and mis-sharing leads to conflict. Consider this: You got wasted while on vacation? Put it on your Facebook page and see what happens. Chumming up with your boys and holding your middle finger up in a picture as a part of the moment? Put it on your Facebook page. Caught in the moment somewhere in a picture with a handsome guy that your boyfriend or husband does not know about? Let it wind up on a Facebook page and see what happens. What you are likely to discover is that oversharing and mis-sharing is a recipe for chaos. Anyone can understand that.

However, even if you understand the possible consequences and you are careful about the information you share, what about what your friends share or even what the friends of your friends share? Are they as careful as you? As if resisting the urge to mis-share and overshare is not enough, you have to consider what someone else may share that you would prefer they would not. What is innocent or funny to one person can be downright embarrassing to another. Also, what about those inevitable pictures that Facebook users get tagged in that they did not want shared? Those pictures can get passed around and viewed by throngs of people in an instant.

Unfortunately, many people don't see the career or professional ramifications of oversharing or mis-sharing online. Some may be familiar with the teacher who was fired by her school because she posted a picture of herself drinking alcohol on her Facebook page. However, they may not recognize the unprofessional impressions they make on their own Facebook pages, impressions that a prospective employer may never share with them directly, yet they affect their careers nonetheless. Today, employers are hiring applicants and colleges are accepting students based in part on those impressions. Again, the employer or school may never share that the person's Facebook page affected their chances of employment or acceptance, but the reality is, it often does.

I even know a guy who was stalked on Facebook, which I am coming to learn is a regular occurrence on Facebook. In his case, a girl he dated trolled through his Facebook friends, contacted other girls who were his "friends," and interrogated them online to see if they were dating him. This bizarre behavior, which could have occurred offline, was made very easy through Facebook because she had access to all his friends. I also had a friend share with me the story of her girlfriend who was being bullied by other women in her network out of jealousy over a guy she was dating. These women were all professional women in their late 30s who waged this online Facebook campaign because of a photo they saw on Facebook of their girl-"friend" apparently dating the ex of another "friend." The perceived protocol violation caused the victim tremendous stress because she was being tormented through the postings and threats these other women were making online. Luckily though, better judgment did prevail as one of the key perpetrators diffused the conflict by apologizing and admitting she was just "following the crowd."

Unfortunately, even in many divorce courts throughout the United States, Facebook is being cited as a key instigator in marital breakups. Online images and content don't just fade away; they can easily re-emerge and cause undue conflict at any time, so I believe it's important not to be a part of oversharing and mis-sharing. If I am to use Facebook, I have to do my best to steer clear of conflict.

Question:

1. Have you ever seen conflict emerge as a result of Facebook or online communication?

2. Have you ever been a part of an online or Facebook conflict?

3. Could the conflict have been prevented by changing the technology's design or the privacy settings? Or could it have been prevented only by changing the perceptions and behavior of the people involved?

CHAPTER SEVENTEEN

Reputation

A wise man once said that a good name is worth more than gold. In business, that good name is called your brand; in life it is called your reputation. It's an unfair fact of life that it takes a lifetime to build a good name and sometimes only seconds to completely destroy one. History is replete with people who destroyed their good reputation in a moment. History is also full of people who had their names destroyed by the false allegations, accusations, and ill intentions of others. When you have a reputation to protect, you can feel the gravity and weight of a tool like Facebook because it gives people the power to affect your name and reputation with everyone you know in seconds.

It's challenging enough to build a good name through responsible living, good decision making, and being a person of sound judgment and character. Yet when the power of your name and reputation is surrendered to the public through a tool like Facebook, that challenge gets even greater. Someone can post something inaccurate, misleading, or even false about you on Facebook, and you are affected because it was shared directly with all your friends. That is not a good thing. There is the assumption of trust and etiquette with social media tools like Facebook. It's like surrendering a measure of control over your reputation to a semipublic mob, rather than having your reputation built solely on the way you live your life. It is one thing to actually do something that could affect your reputation; it's another thing for someone to simply post something about you that actually affects your reputation.

Now I can see why many celebrities resent blogs and the tabloids. Nameless and faceless people can post or say anything about them, all of which affect the public's perception of them and forces them to have to decide whether or not to respond to it. And with its voyeuristic design, Facebook invites everyone to look into your life and comment on it, leaving a running narrative online of the collective perception others have of you and your postings. That is a lot of trust.

The question I have to ask myself is, "Should everyone in my network have access to my entire network?" I don't think so. Having that kind of access is a measure of power that may be too generous. Furthermore, I value my time too much to waste it reacting to some frivolous digital postings or to try to manage an online identity. I see countless people on Facebook spending their real time reacting to stuff they would not ordinarily react to, not realizing that just reacting to these postings changes you and how you are perceived.

Recently an old buddy of mine who is a college professor made a remark about a mutual friend who he said was always on Facebook offering and responding to silly postings. He said to me, "Mike, what happened to D? He has become a bit of a dumb ass." I responded that I thought it was a Facebook thing and that the guy was likely just as sharp as ever. It was interesting to me that a guy's reputation was being redefined by how he participated in Facebook chatter.

Then there is my friend "J," who felt slightly embarrassed because his old friends shared things on his page that no longer reflected who he was and all his other "friends" saw those postings. The experience made him uncomfortable because his current friends' perception of him was being affected by these old friends and their postings. Yet offline, in the real world, this would never have been an issue because the old friends and the new friends would not have access to one another. The old friends would remain a part of his past and the new friends would be in his current reality. However, through Facebook, his old friends had access to all his Facebook friends and thus had the ability to influence his current life. In the end, J chose to do what many other Facebook users do under similar circumstances: He "de-friended" his older friends. Of course they were offended, and consequently their relationship with him changed and they no longer consider him a good friend. Sadly, none of them wanted this outcome, and it was all avoidable. It was merely the result of Facebook's inadequate design—a design that blurs the line between past and present and ignores the personal and sometimes private nature of all communication by making communication public, not only to their friends, but even to their friends' friends. Maybe opening oneself and one's life up like that to everyone is a massive surrender to the group.

I hold that the power to define one's self has to remain with the individual. And by placing everyone you have known in the same place and giving them all access to your life, your relationships, and your communication, you surrender too much of that power. I think people should begin to recognize, value, and exercise their power to define themselves and not surrender it to an online crowd. This will likely be a challenge I will have to navigate if I am to plunge into the world of Facebook.

Questions:

1. Do you think your reputation or image is affected or shaped in any way by others with whom you are connected to or communicate with online?

2. What do your Facebook page, your Facebook postings, and the postings of your Facebook "friends" say about you?

3. Have you ever felt the negative impact of people having access to your Facebook "friends" or your communication?

4. Has your reputation ever been affected online by other people?

FREE GIFT MA'AM!
FREE GIFT!

CHAPTER EIGHTEEN

Free Gift!

A few years ago there was a guy who worked at a vending table in my local mall. I imagine he worked for a credit card company or a data collection company because I could see applications on his table. What was hilarious was he had these intense, bulging eyes, and I could not get within 20 yards of him without him shouting, "Free gift, sir! Free gift!!" In fact, no one was exempt; everyone could get it. "Free gift, ma'am. Free gift!" He was a bit obnoxious and aggressive. He was determined to give you that free gift if you gave him your personal information. I haven't seen him in the mall now for years, nor have I seen those cars on display that were supposedly raffled off to those who completed a contestant form. I suspect they have all gone the way of the dinosaur because who needs companies like that when you have a company like Facebook? "Free gift, ma'am! Free gift!!"

It's surprising how much personal information people will share with a company when the company gives them something for free. Hundreds of millions of people are online sharing all their personal data, consumer habits, opinions, and every bit of information that is relevant in their lives all because they are completely enamored with the "free gift." In this case, the free gift is the amazing global communication tool known as Facebook. It is a personal data collection company's Shangri-La. I guess for these past few years I have been leery of Facebook just like I was leery of the guy in the mall, knowing that if I was getting something that good for free, there had to be a catch.

I suppose the saying is true: In business nothing is truly free; somebody is paying for it somewhere. What appears to be free is in fact not free. Instead, in the case of Facebook, there is simply confusion over what the product being sold actually is. Most Facebook users assume the product is the site, while in fact the product is ultimately them and all their data, communications, and friends.

Essentially, the thing that makes Facebook unique is that the user is the product.

Questions:

1. Have you ever accepted a company's offer of a "free gift"?

2. If so, were you aware of what you gave the company in return?

3. Can you see how Facebook could be perceived as a "free gift" offer?

CHAPTER NINETEEN

Nothing Personal, Just Business

But what about all the assurances that my data will always remain private and will never be sold? Well, I do believe that is true, at least in the near future, but only if properly understood. Who would really want to buy my personal pictures anyhow? The fact is that the important information is not the individual *per se*; it's in the patterns of the individual's data or the interpretation of the data. So when Facebook says it won't sell my data, that is different from saying Facebook will not compile a consumer profile based on all my data and sell access to that information and access to me. For example, who really cares if Sharon from Ohio said in a posting she likes the new 300 series BMW? However, when 800 people make similar remarks, a pattern can be developed around all their personal information and demographics. Then, using all of this data, Facebook can compile consumer profiles and create valuable statistics that they use to sell targeted advertising or possibly to sell access to the data's interpretation. In essence, this makes Facebook the greatest market research tool in history. It is a company whose value is determined not only by the number of users and time spent on the site, but by its data collection, data analytics, and data mining capabilities. All that market research is used for precisely targeted advertising and could also be used for other business purposes.

Facebook is similar to the guy in the mall, except that by accepting Facebook as the free gift, you don't get junk mail sent to your home like you would for completing the guy's application. Instead, you see ads based on your information in the margins of your Facebook page, or maybe you have to tolerate personalized ads while you surf other websites. At worst, maybe some company or agency will buy access to the demographics for your consumer habits or buy access to your anonymous consumer profile.

In either case, I am of the opinion that I own my personal experiences, preferences, communication, and data, though Facebook would have me believe it is all community property (their community). Ironically, Facebook itself is a private company that does not share its operational details with its users. Users don't know for sure if any agencies and companies purchase access to their data analytics or consumer statistics, nor do they know how that data is being used and shared. Users also do not know if information that is generated or gathered when utilizing a Facebook application and/or game is adequately protected by the third-party company that created and administered the application.

Could it be that the company, which demands openness from all of its users, may not follow its own rule? Is the default setting social for Facebook also? The bottom line is that on Facebook, nothing is truly personal; it is all business. With that in mind, on May 18, 2012, Facebook was sold to the public and is now accountable to shareholders and profits. This begs the question: Will one's data always remain private? For now, the answer appears to be "yes" as Mark Zuckerberg is the major stockholder, but what about in the future?

In using Facebook I can't be naïve. It is a business and everything on the site is for that purpose.

Questions:

1. Do you care if people profit off the use of your personal data and communication?

2. If a company like Facebook provides you with entertainment, a means of connecting with others, and convenience in return for the use of your personal communication and data, is that a fair trade?

CHAPTER TWENTY

Gradual Change

What happens a few years from now when the whole Facebook community is acculturated to the norm of sharing everything much like its founder desires? At that point no one would care if their personal information was shared. They would agree with the edict that the default setting is social. Under those circumstances, the whole Facebook community would have undergone a slow gradual change that was hardly noticeable. They would have drifted into a new reality where all information, personal or otherwise, was completely open without a thought for privacy or personal boundaries. By then, many people would have grown up in this culture, assuming it was the only or best way to live. At that point, people would willingly share all their personal information, and no one would have any objections to it because of the way they had been conditioned over time. Is this the eventual goal? That people will get used to it?

Well, I don't want to move in that direction. I happen to believe that some things are too valuable to be commercialized. Additionally, if something of mine is to be sold, I want to be paid for it, and I will determine what is sold and how much it is sold for. I am not going to give up everything that is precious to me—my memories, my communication, my relationships, and my experiences—for free, only for someone else to turn around and sell them. After all, it stands to reason that if the company that owns my communication and personal experiences was sold, all my personal information was part of the transaction. Isn't the data and user base Facebook's biggest asset? Of course it is. It also means that if the company ever ends up valued at $100 billion and there are roughly one billion users, each user's information could be viewed as worth roughly $100.

Questions about personal information and how it is gathered and shared are huge ethical issues that I think are worthy of consideration. Privacy is one issue, but there is also the issue of someone creating and selling access to me and my personal data, while in return I get only a virtual environment in which they can observe me and collect data. The thought of it makes me feel a little bit like a lab rat. Should I allow someone to compile sets of data analytics off my precious personal life, profit from it, and make themselves billions of dollars, while in return I get no compensation?

I don't think so. Somehow I have to receive benefit beyond simply chatting it up with friends.

Questions:

1. Do you think Facebook has a long-term strategy and end goal regarding the use of its users' data?

2. Do you think the Facebook strategy is to condition its users to no longer view personal privacy as a concern?

IS BIG BROTHER WATCHING YOU?

CHAPTER TWENTY-ONE

Big Brother

In 1949, a very popular novel entitled *1984* was published. In brief, the novel is about a society that on the surface appeared to be utopian—peaceful and perfect—while in reality it was a repressive state that used brainwashing, propaganda, and universal surveillance to control its citizens. Over time, the book came to symbolize government surveillance and imposition upon its citizens, which later gave rise to the popular expression that "Big brother is watching you." It also embodied the concerns of some civil rights advocates, activists, and dissident groups in the United States who feared the escalation and potential abuse of government surveillance. Concerns about the use of domestic spying and its potential abuses have been a part of the American discourse since the days of Jay Edgar Hoover and the FBI and continue today with terrorism-prevention tactics. As such, the specter of a government Big Brother appears to have yet to materialize due to public concerns.

On the contrary, it is corporations that are in the business of covertly—or perhaps not so covertly—gathering personal information. For example, you use your rewards card and all your buying habits are recorded and stored with data collection companies. You innocently play a free online game, and spyware is secretly downloaded to your computer, tracking all your computer activities and sharing that information with the company that created the game. I'm sure everyone who is online has heard of spyware.

Is Facebook glorified spyware?

In November of 2007, Facebook triggered an uproar when it rolled out its Beacon program. Designed to increase openness and sharing, Beacon tracked your purchases with other partnering websites and shared that information with all your friends on your profile page. What further angered people was the fact that the feature was automatic, requiring you to opt out as opposed to opting in. As a result of the uproar, the program was modified to opt in, and the program's name was changed to Facebook Connect, from what I understand.

Now, new features such as "instant personalization" also infringe upon the user in similar ways. From what I know, once a user logs onto a website with their Facebook login, those sites will have access to all their Facebook data to create a "personalized experience" for them when they are on those websites. It is similar to what Pandora Radio does when making radio suggestions, except it uses the person's Facebook data to suggest product recommendations. The implications of this are that people's profiles and data are being shared with companies that use it to pitch them, or rather to improve their buying experience.

Also under "instant personalization," Facebook, as the gateway to your web experience, will also have your "clickstream" or browsing history while you are on the web. Zuckerberg made a statement in a recent television interview that Facebook wants to create a world "where every product experience is social and covered through Facebook." This means every product purchase or opinion would be facilitated through Facebook and shared far and wide. This statement begs the question, "If all the product experiences of a billion-plus people are shared and facilitated through Facebook, along with all their relationships, ideas, photos, memories, thoughts, and experiences, does that ultimately anoint Zuckerberg and Facebook as Big Brother? Does that type of arrangement confine billions of people in a virtual closed environment called Facebook, where they are monitored and manipulated like Jim Carrey's character in *The Truman Show*?" Maybe it does. Maybe it doesn't. In either case it sure is a hell of a lot of trust and power to surrender to one person or company.

Even if the United States government is a potential "Big Brother," the government is still technically accountable to the people and to its founding documents. However, private corporations are required to answer only to their shareholders and to generate profits, which means private corporations can do things government agencies simply cannot. Ultimately free enterprise means there is very little government oversight and regulation over these massive corporations like Facebook.

So as smart and as competent as Zuckerberg and his team have proven themselves to be, I think that level of trust and power is largely unearned and eventually likely to be corrupting. Surrendering that much power to one man and his company exalts Facebook to a godlike status that requires more than technical savvy and corporate genius as prerequisites. Among many other things, I think it necessitates a deep philosophical reservoir of insight into human beings, society, and history. It also demands impeccable personal and corporate ethics and controls, along with a profound respect for all individuals, their rights, and their needs. And lastly it demands public vigilance because as it is often stated, "Absolute power corrupts absolutely." I am not sure I see these things yet.

Ironically, on a side note, a gentleman who is in information technology informed me that corporations always leave a back door open in their computer systems for government agencies to access their data. This suggests that in either case, corporate or government, a bigger brother is in some ways always watching. This does not mean everyone is a criminal, or even that everyone has something to hide, but the reality of a "Big Brother" watching is something to consider when sharing online.

Questions:

1. Do you find the idea of a "Big Brother" watching you discomforting and creepy, or of no concern at all?

2. Do you think Facebook is becoming like "Big Brother" to its hundreds of millions of users?

3. Do you have a concern that a corporation like Facebook can amass too much personal information and influence over people's lives?

JUST WHEN I THOUGHT
I WAS OUT...
THEY PULLED ME BACK IN.

CHAPTER TWENTY-TWO

Mob Life

"Just when I thought I was out, they pull me back in." I love that line from *The Godfather: Part III.* It characterizes something that is often said about the criminal lifestyle: Once you are in the life, it is almost impossible to get out. This also appears true of Facebook. In movies, you often see criminal figures using personal relationships to manipulate their targets. The offer goes something like this: "You know, we wouldn't want any harm to come your family." It's classic manipulation. Well, Facebook apparently uses a far more benign, but equally manipulative version of the same tactic. Upon trying to delete your Facebook account, you are sent pictures from Facebook of your friends and family that are going to miss you. It is not that these particular people actually sent you the message, nor that they even care if you delete your account; rather it is Facebook using their names and images to give you the impression they will miss you—classic manipulation. If you are able to overcome this tactic and avoid the feelings of guilt it is intended to create, you face yet another problem: How do you permanently delete your account?

Facebook does not make it easy. I have a friend who created a Facebook profile a few years ago that she never used and later deleted it. Years later she opened another account, which she uses regularly. Only now she is faced with having two accounts because the one she deleted came back and will not go away. It occasionally pops up when she logs in. Like in a classic slasher film, she just can't seem to kill her first profile. It just won't die and it won't go away. Another friend of mine expressed similar frustration in trying to permanently delete his account. He enjoyed a chuckle when, like ghosts, several of his friends appeared in a message to him that said, "The following people will miss you."

Obviously there is a way to permanently delete your account, but you really have to know what you're doing. Facebook, however, does reserve the right to store your information, even after you close your account. This means you could technically have a profile that lives on forever, well beyond you, and if the profile was reactivated with an administrator, it could continue to accumulate friends, communicate, and build relationships even when you're dead.

I know that's a pretty eerie thought, but it is actually not that far from reality because once you are on Facebook, Facebook owns your profile, and technically through them you can live on. In the end the company doesn't even need you to profit; it just needs your data.

Questions:

1. Have you or anyone you know tried to delete their Facebook account?
2. Is the page actually deleted or just inactive?
3. Have you ever thought of deleting your Facebook account?
4. If so why?

CHAPTER TWENTY-THREE

Extraordinary Popular Delusions and the Madness of Crowds

Are we looking at technological wonders, or should we wonder about how we use technology?

Improved technology, which gave us microwave ovens and fast food, in turn contributed to increases in obesity and poor nutrition. Virtually everyone's favorite technology, cable television and the remote control, have led many of us down the slippery slope of complacency and laziness. The point is, with any new technology there are always unforeseen or unintended consequences. This should not make us so fearful that we turn back, but rather it should make us aware, reflective, and thoughtful about how we engage the increasing proliferation of life-altering technologies. There are a great number of questions that can be raised regarding the psychological and societal implications resulting from the widespread use of social networking tools like Facebook, questions, which to varying degrees are quite relevant. Here are just a few:

1. What are the implications of people creating a digital representation of themselves and relating through these profiles?

2. Does it provide a false sense of self? Does it provide a false sense of confidence, courage, and social competence online that people are unable to express when in person?

3. Does it provide a cop-out for the shy and socially awkward, such that they are never challenged to develop real social skills?

4. Does it feed on our insecurities or our need for attention?

5. Does it feed our need to be liked?

6. Does it actually isolate us through shallow digital communication and thus invariably lead to a sense of loneliness?

7. Does it make us and our relationships a little less authentic?

Everyone has to admit that it is much easier to post or say something online than it is to actually stand in the presence of others and say it or represent it. The same person who can't speak in front of a crowd can type online in the presence of thousands. I have observed similar dynamics on many occasions, particularly when hiring a new employee. On paper someone can shine like a star, while in person during the interview they can completely bomb. Then there are those who interview well, but once on the job their dysfunction and incompetence emerge. It appears that by giving the user a false sense of social competence and self-efficacy, that some social-networking tools actually create an illusory social reality even while purporting to foster real connections.

Then there is the power of group dynamics. In popular terms it is known as "groupthink." It is an undeniable, well-documented scientific fact that individual behavior is altered when in a group dynamic. When belonging to a group, most individuals will do or say what they think is agreeable to the group. In extreme cases, individuals will even do what they feel is morally wrong and reprehensible when the activity is supported by a group and/or authority figure. Though it is an extreme example, it points to the power of the group on individual behavior. The phenomenon of groupthink automatically emerges when people operate in groups. The fact is that people do change when in the presence of or under the watchful eye of the group. It is natural, and Facebook is a groupthink phenomenon.

As a result of the impact of groupthink, I see many Facebook users changing subtlety and gradually. People who were not gossipers begin to gossip. Folks who were not voyeuristic begin taking great pleasure in following someone else's life. Folks who had personal boundaries and who led fairly private lives gradually become open books. The power of groupthink is real, and with the huge popularity of Facebook, groupthink leads to the emergence of new social norms based on new values and priorities. For example, Facebook's promotion of openness, transparency, and the sharing of personal information with everyone is a complete cultural shift in human behavior and identity. Much like Christianity has forgiveness and the doing of good as its core principles, Facebook appears to have sharing (personal information) as the core value of its culture.

Zuckerberg has said that the mission of Facebook is to "give people the power to share and to make the world more open and connected." I think that sounds wonderful and is a noble goal; however, as things appear now, the reality of Facebook's legacy may actually wind up being that it gradually furthered our descent into narcissism, egotism, voyeurism, exhibitionism, and immaturity, thus making everyone a "Bookface." I hope this will not be the case and is why I wrote *Bookface*—to raise questions and spark a dialogue about how Facebook affects who we are, how we relate, and how we utilize our precious time.

Questions:

1. Do you see "groupthink" at work on Facebook?

2. Do you even care?

CHAPTER TWENTY-FOUR

So What's Good?

In all fairness, with all that I have written in the previous chapters, Facebook is a global communication tool of epic proportions. It facilitates relationships and communication everywhere, and in that regard its potential mirrors our collective potential, which is limitless. As is true of any tool or technology, it merely does what we use it to do. Most people use Facebook responsibly. Friends and family connect and share. Businesses and brands relate to their customers. Celebrities keep in touch with their fan base. People play all sorts of fun and interesting games. Its positive utility is the reason it has over 800 million users. Facebook and social media have indeed changed the world. People spend so much time on Facebook because it is fun and entertaining. It facilitates business, and for most users it's free. How amazing is that? There are many moving stories of how people have connected with loved ones and reconnected with friends from their past. I know of several people who have met the love of their life on Facebook, and that is truly beautiful. Even social causes have been advanced using Facebook as a tool, as was the case with the "Arab Spring revolutions."

Recently, Facebook introduced many new socially responsible features, such as organ donation, and there are likely many more such features to follow. Plans for the improved facilitation of e-commerce are already underway. As a platform for coders to develop applications, Facebook creates many job opportunities and is an almost-limitless ecosystem.

I can only applaud the sheer genius of Mark Zuckerberg and his team. Their vision and tenacity has improved the lives of many millions of people. I look forward to the further evolution of social media tools, including Facebook. The future is truly exciting.

Questions:

1. What do you like most about Facebook?
2. What features do you use most on Facebook?
3. How has using Facebook improved your quality of life?

Conclusion

A process which began as a Facebook critique ended up being a journey of personal growth and transformation. I set out to explore the psychological and sociological implications of Facebook, and in the process I explored myself. It proved to be a wonderful learning experience. If, as a result of this process, I was able to provide some insights regarding Facebook and our use of social media tools as well as raise some important questions, then my journey has been that much better. I do believe we have to be thoughtful about how major societal changes affect us. No technology is perfect.

For every technology of good, there are often negative applications or unintended consequences. As we are all delighted to have cable television with a remote control, we have to admit it greatly contributes to our collective laziness and is partly responsible for the "couch potato" phenomenon. As amazing as video games are, we now know that with the exception of motion detection video games, the video gaming industry has played a major role in the rise of childhood obesity as kids everywhere watch screens rather than physically play outside.

For me, the insights I gained while writing *Bookface* deepened my appreciation for the huge impact others can have upon you in a social-networking environment. Even with all the hoopla around social media tools like Facebook, those tools don't change the nature of people nor how they impact your life. It's a reality that I believe has to be appreciated. Most folks intend good, while only a small percentage of people are mischief makers; however, under certain circumstances, even those who intend good can intentionally or unintentionally cause mischief, and social media tools can greatly empower them to do so. Therefore, until we belong to a society where our character, ethics, and morals are such that we use empathy, good judgment, and discipline to control ourselves from taking advantage of or harming others, we have to be wise enough to protect ourselves from each other. This also includes being aware of surrendering to much of ourselves to institutions, corporations, and governments and inadvertently putting ourselves at risk for being taken advantage of. I acknowledge that for many this is a very touchy subject, but it is worthy of mention. Euphoria around social media tools should not make us naïve or irrational.

In addition, because social media tools are here to stay, we have to develop a way to use them wisely and responsibly. When I discussed some of my concerns with my good friend James Power, he shared with me a code he tries to follow when on Facebook and other social media sites. I felt the code could be of benefit to others, so I'm sharing it here. He calls it the 5 Gs. It goes like this: When you're on Facebook or other social media sites, conduct yourself as if ...

- your **G**randmother
- your **G**irlfriend or **G**uy friend

- the **G**overnment
- **G**angsters
- **G**od

are all watching and listening. At first it sounded a little over the top, but when I thought about it, it made a lot of sense. Here is the breakdown of the 5 G code for online conduct:

- Acting as if **G**randma is watching would generally mean you would always respect yourself and others.
- Acting as if your **G**irl or **G**uy friend is watching would keep you from doing things that would create relationship trouble.
- Acting as if the **G**overnment is watching would ensure you shared nothing illegal or that could be perceived as such.
- Acting as if **G**angsters are watching is simply a way of saying be aware that criminals are online too, so watch what you share.
- Acting as if **G**od is watching means you don't share something you may one day regret.

Following this code can create a sense of awareness and responsibility in a person who cares. In fact, many people already follow it instinctively. As a guide for online conduct, I think it can help prevent oversharing and mis-sharing. Ultimately when online we have to be conscious of the bigger picture and know our limits. Carelessness is the doorway to regret.

In the end, on a personal note, I still have to answer whether or not I will get a Facebook page. And all things considered, I guess my answer is yes, but not so much for social use. Facebook is way too powerful a tool for me to sit on the sidelines and not utilize it. After having gone through the process of writing this book, I know how I can use Facebook without compromising who I am. I needed to articulate my views before I could I join, and I am really gratified by the personal insights I have gained. Confronting Facebook really helped me confront myself. In a strange way it ended up being a therapeutic process. Not only did I clarify my boundaries and my values, I came to better understand how one of my hang-ups has impacted my life. This realization has inspired me to make some changes.

It also gave me clarity about how to use Facebook in a responsible way. Will this mean that my life is now an open book? Not likely. Tools like Facebook are here to serve our purposes, but they don't have to change us in ways we don't want.

We are not a collection of commercialized digital data snippets. We are far more than that.

And speaking of myself, I can say that I doubt I will ever be a Bookface, but I can't say that I didn't create one.

Thank you for reading my little book.

Thank you to Mark Zuckerberg and his Facebook team for providing the world with an amazing global network and communication tool.

You set out to change the world and the world will never be the same.

Final questions for consideration:

1. What affect do you think social media tools like Facebook have on people's lives and behaviors?

2. Do you think there is merit in the observations and opinions that were expressed about Facebook in this book?

3. Do you agree with any of the points that were made in this book?

4. Do you feel this book will affect your perception, conduct, or use of social media tools like Facebook?

5. If so, how?

ARE YOU SURE YOU DON'T WANT ANY COOL AID?
WELL, MAYBE JUST A SIP...

Let's keep in touch

The work of Michael Billion is a progressive strategic rollout of ideas, institutions, projects, and creative works designed to impact the world for the better. We would be honored if you stayed in touch with us and joined the movement to change the world for the better.

Visit: www.MichaelBillion.com

Follow the author on Twitter: @MBillion

Facebook: Michael Billion

Email Michael: mikebillion@gmail.com

Join the Bookface conversation at:
Facebook.com/Bookface
#Bookface

Coming soon from the author is *A Billion Changes: Our Roadmap for Changing the World. A Billion Changes* is a breakthrough book that reveals Michael's strategy for how we will permanently change the world for the better.

Don't miss out on this game-changing book.

Made in the USA
Monee, IL
04 November 2026

67376425R00066